CONTENTS

Introduction

Thanks for picking up this book. By baking you can help make a big difference to the lives of people in the UK and Africa.

Nothing beats a tasty treat, so this **Red Nose Day**, on **Friday 15 March 2013**, why not bake something yummy for money? The 13 bakes in this collection are all simple to make, so anyone can have a go.

We've put together some helpful tips on hosting your own bake sale, so just turn the page to get started.

You've already contributed £2 to Comic Relief by buying this book. If you'd like more inspiration and information about how you can help change lives this Red Nose Day, see page 5.

Happy baking!

How to host a bake sale

Tips for a showstopping bake sale

- Time your bake sale to when people will want a nibble wherever you are, for example during break times, lunch or afternoon tea.
- People will be more likely to buy extra treats if they can carry them home, so keep some containers or paper bags handy.
- You've worked hard on your bakes, so be sure to make a profit. If you spend £10 on ingredients, try to take at least £30 in sales.
- A good way to make even more money at your bake sale is to organise a raffle. You could ask local food producers to donate prizes.
- Get as many people as possible to come along by creating an attraction like a 'just for fun' record attempt. How about the tallest sponge tower?
- Cake eating is thirsty work, so serving tea and coffee alongside your bakes always appeals. And remember some soft drinks for the kids, too.
- Here's a sneaky little tip for a good cause – don't price your cakes. People may pay more for something if they don't know its price.
- Hold onto a list of your ingredients in case anyone has any allergies. You could label nut-free bakes with a little sign.
- Don't forget to have plenty of loose change available at your sale.

How you can change lives

If you put on your own bake sale this **Red Nose Day,** you could help make a big difference to people living unimaginably tough lives in the UK and across Africa.

What sort of difference?, you ask
This sort:

£25 could provide a therapy session for a child in the UK who has suffered neglect and abuse to help them cope with their traumatic experience.

£50 could keep a child in Uganda safe, sheltered, fed and off the streets for a whole month.

£100 could enable 8 children who used to work in the gold mines of Ghana to attend basic literacy classes, giving them the chance to go to school and work towards a brighter future.

£25

£50

£100

English Summer Cupcakes

These cupcakes are filled with fresh strawberries and strawberry jam and finished with a piped swirl of sweet cream-cheese frosting – delicious.

Makes 12 cupcakes

FOR THE SPONGE MIXTURE

125g unsalted butter, at room temperature

175g caster sugar

2 large eggs, at room temperature

½ teaspoon vanilla extract

175g self-raising flour

good pinch of salt

3 tablespoons milk, at room temperature

100g hulled strawberries, cut into small pieces

1–2 tablespoons strawberry jam

FOR THE FROSTING

125g unsalted butter, at room temperature

250g full-fat cream cheese

½ teaspoon vanilla extract

275g icing sugar, sifted

strawberries, to decorate

1 Preheat the oven to 180°C/350°F/gas 4. Line a 12-hole muffin tray with paper cupcake or muffin cases. If you want to pipe the icing, you will also need a piping bag fitted with a star tube.

2 Put the butter into a large mixing bowl and beat using a wooden spoon or an electric mixer for 1 minute or until creamy. Gradually beat in the sugar and keep beating for 4–5 minutes until very light and fluffy.

3 Beat the eggs with the vanilla, then add to the creamed mixture a tablespoon at a time, beating well after each addition and scraping down the sides of the bowl from time to time. Sift the flour and salt into the bowl, add the milk and gently fold together using a large metal spoon. Gently fold in the chopped strawberries.

4 Spoon the mixture into the paper cases, dividing it evenly. Bake for 20 minutes until risen, golden brown and firm to the touch. Remove the tray from the oven and cool for about 2 minutes, then carefully transfer the cupcakes to a wire rack and cool completely.

5 Using the tip of a small, sharp knife, remove a small cone of sponge from the middle of each cake. Add about ¼ teaspoon of strawberry jam to each small hole, then replace the plug of sponge.

6 To make the frosting, beat together the butter, cream cheese and vanilla until soft and creamy, using an electric mixer or a wooden spoon. Gradually beat in the icing sugar (on low speed if using an electric mixer). Spoon the frosting into the piping bag and pipe a swirl on top of each cupcake or smooth the icing over each cake using a round-bladed knife. Decorate with a whole or halved strawberry, if you like. Eat the same day.

Squidgy Brownies

Really good brownies are irresistible, and these have melted chocolate and cocoa for a fudgy flavour and texture. You can add your own extras – nuts, or even more chocolate.

Cuts into 20 pieces

200g unsalted butter, cut into sticks

100g bar dark chocolate, broken into pieces

200g caster sugar

4 eggs, at room temperature

½ teaspoon vanilla extract

75g plain flour

25g cocoa powder

100g your choice of extras: walnut or pecan pieces OR white, dark or milk choc chips

1 Preheat the oven to 180°C/350°F/gas 4. Grease a 20.5 x 30.5cm traybake tin and line the base with baking paper.

2 Put the butter in a saucepan with the broken chocolate. Set the pan over the lowest possible heat and leave the butter and chocolate to melt gently, stirring every minute or so with a wooden spoon. Take the pan off the heat as soon as the mixture is smooth and set aside.

3 Put the sugar, eggs and vanilla essence into a mixing bowl. Beat with a wire whisk or an electric mixer for 2 minutes until thoroughly combined and the mixture is slightly frothy.

4 Pour the melted chocolate into the bowl and whisk it in for a minute until you can no longer see any streaks of dark brown.

5 Sift the flour and cocoa into another bowl. Stir into the chocolate mixture with the wooden spoon (there's no need to wash it). When everything is combined, stir in your choice of extras, distributing them evenly.

6 Scrape the mixture into the prepared tin and spread evenly right into the corners. Gently bang the tin on the worktop to knock out pockets of air.

7 Carefully place in the preheated oven and bake for 20 minutes. To test if the brownie is cooked, push a skewer into the centre of the cake. If it comes out clean, the cake is ready; if necessary, bake for 2 more minutes and test again.

8 Set the tin on a wire rack and leave to cool before cutting into squares. Store in an airtight container and eat within 5 days.

Sticky Orange Marmalade Cake

A really good Seville orange marmalade – home-made or a top brand – one with an intense bittersweet flavour plus decent chunks of peel, transforms a simple creamed sponge mixture into an old-fashioned treat.

Makes 1 medium cake

FOR THE SPONGE

175g unsalted butter, at room temperature

175g caster sugar

3 large eggs, at room temperature, beaten

175g self-raising flour

pinch of salt

½ level teaspoon baking powder

3 level tablespoons chunky Seville orange marmalade

2 tablespoons full-fat or semi-skimmed milk

TO FINISH

3 level tablespoons chunky Seville orange marmalade

100g icing sugar

2 tablespoons warm water

1 Preheat the oven to 180°C/350°F/gas 4. Grease a 20cm round, springclip or deep round cake tin and line the base with baking paper.

2 Put the butter into a large mixing bowl and beat with a wooden spoon or electric mixer for 1 minute or until creamy. Gradually beat in the sugar, and keep beating for 4–5 minutes until very light and fluffy.

3 Gradually add the eggs, beating well after each addition; add a tablespoon of the flour with the last portion of egg. Sift the remaining flour, the salt and baking powder into the bowl and gently fold into the mixture using a large metal spoon. When thoroughly combined add the marmalade and milk and stir in.

4 Spoon the mixture into the prepared tin and spread evenly. Bake for 50–55 minutes or until a good golden brown and firm to the touch. Run a round-bladed knife around the inside of the tin to loosen the cake, then carefully turn out onto a wire rack.

5 Gently warm the second portion of marmalade and brush over the top of the warm cake. Leave to cool completely.

6 Sift the icing sugar into a bowl, add the warm water and mix to a smooth, runny icing using a wooden spoon. Spoon the icing over the cake and let it run down the sides – the chunks of marmalade will stick up through the icing. Leave until set before cutting. Store in an airtight container and eat within 5 days.

Stem Ginger Shortbread

Good butter is the key to a wonderful taste here, while a combination of plain flour and either rice flour, ground rice or cornflour gives the crisp, short (but not tough) texture.

Makes 20

200g unsalted butter, at room temperature

100g caster sugar, plus extra for sprinkling

260g plain flour

40g rice flour, ground rice or cornflour

½ level teaspoon ground ginger

good pinch of salt

50g stem ginger, chopped small

1 Grease two baking sheets. Put the butter into a large mixing bowl and beat using a wooden spoon or an electric mixer until creamy. Gradually beat in the sugar and keep beating for 4–5 minutes until very light and fluffy.

2 Sift the flour with the rice flour (or ground rice or cornflour), ground ginger and salt into the bowl. Add the chopped ginger and work all the ingredients together with your hands until thoroughly combined. Form the dough into a log shape about 20cm long and wrap in clingfilm. Chill for 20–30 minutes or until firm.

3 Preheat the oven to 170°C/325°F/gas 3. Unwrap the log and slice across into 20 rounds using a large sharp knife. Arrange slightly apart on the prepared baking sheets (or bake in batches if you only have one baking sheet).

4 Bake for about 20 minutes or until firm but not coloured. Remove from the oven and sprinkle with caster sugar, then leave on the baking sheets to cool and firm up for a couple of minutes. Transfer to a wire rack and leave to cool completely. Store in an airtight container and eat within a week.

Sticky Confetti Cake

A flat sheet of sponge can be turned into any number of different cakes – perfect for big parties, bake sales and school fairs.

Cuts into 20 pieces

125g unsalted butter, at room temperature

125g caster sugar

2 eggs, at room temperature

150g self-raising flour

1 tablespoon milk

1 teaspoon vanilla extract

5 tablespoons coloured sugar hundreds-and-thousands OR sugar strands OR coloured sweets

FOR THE ICING

250g icing sugar

100g unsalted butter, at room temperature

1 tablespoon milk

1 Preheat the oven to 180°C/350°F/gas 4. Grease a 20.5 x 25.5 x 5cm traybake tin and line the base with baking paper.

2 Put the butter and sugar into a large mixing bowl. Add the eggs, flour, milk and vanilla. Beat everything together using a wooden spoon or an electric mixer until very smooth and even in colour. Stop and scrape down the sides of the bowl from time to time. Add 2 tablespoons of the coloured sweeties and mix them in.

3 Scrape the mixture into the prepared tin and spread evenly, right into the corners. Place in the preheated oven and bake for 20–25 minutes until the top is golden brown and the cake is starting to shrink away from the sides of the tin. The cake is cooked if it springs back when gently pressed; if necessary, bake for 2–3 more minutes, then test again.

4 Remove the tin from the oven and set on a wire rack. Loosen the cake in the tin, then leave to cool for 20 minutes. Remove from the tin, peel off the baking paper and leave to cool completely.

5 To make the icing, sift the icing sugar into the washed (and dried) mixing bowl. Add the butter and milk and beat well using the washed wooden spoon or an electric mixer on low speed, until very smooth and paler in colour. Sprinkle the remaining sweeties into the mixture and stir in.

6 Spread the icing over the surface of the cold cake using a round-bladed table knife. Leave to firm up in a cool spot before cutting into squares, slices or rectangles. Store in an airtight container in a cool spot (not the fridge) and eat within 4 days.

Carrot Cake Muffins

You can have all the delicious flavours and textures of carrot cake in a muffin, plus the sweet cream cheese icing as a surprise filling.

Makes 12 cakes

75g shredded bran cereal

225ml milk

zest of 1 medium orange

120g cream cheese

1 level tablespoon caster sugar

3 large carrots

125g light brown muscovado sugar

200g self-raising flour

1 level teaspoon baking powder

1½ level teaspoons ground cinnamon

1 level teaspoon ground ginger

2 eggs

4 tablespoons sunflower oil

1 Put the bran cereal and milk into a large mixing bowl and stir just to mix. Leave to soak for 15 minutes. Meanwhile, preheat the oven to 220°C/425°F/gas 7. Line a 12-hole muffin tray with paper muffin cases.

2 Tip half the zest into the mixing bowl with the cereal and milk and put to one side. Add the cream cheese and caster sugar to the remaining zest in a small bowl and mix well – this will be your filling.

3 Peel the carrots and, using the coarse-hole side of a grater, grate the carrots onto a board. Weigh out 150g grated carrot and add to the large bowl. (Save any leftover carrots for a salad.)

4 By now the cereal will be very mushy. Add the brown sugar and mix well using a wooden spoon. Sift in the flour, baking powder, cinnamon and ginger but don't mix them in just yet.

5 Break the eggs into another bowl and add the oil. Beat with a fork just until the egg yolks are broken up and mixed with the whites. Tip into a mixing bowl and mix everything together with the wooden spoon.

6 Using a medium-sized spoon, drop a dollop of the carrot mixture into each paper muffin case in the tray. Drop a small spoonful of the cream cheese filling into the middle.

7 Cover the filling with the rest of the carrot mixture, dividing it evenly among the cases. Place in the preheated oven and bake for about 20 minutes until golden brown. Check the muffins are cooked by gently pressing the centre of one with your finger – if it springs back then it's ready.

8 Remove the tray from the oven and leave for 5 minutes, then carefully transfer the muffins to a wire rack to cool completely. Store in an airtight container and eat within 24 hours.

Mocha Marble Loaf Cake

This rich chocolate and coffee sponge mixture is studded with chocolate chips and topped with a rich, creamy white chocolate ganache. Dust with cocoa powder for a cappuccino-style finish.

Makes 1 medium loaf cake

250g unsalted butter, at room temperature

250g caster sugar

1 teaspoon vanilla extract

4 large eggs, at room temperature, beaten

250g self-raising flour

good pinch of salt

2–3 tablespoons milk (optional)

FOR THE CHOCOLATE MIXTURE

30g cocoa powder

2 tablespoons milk

FOR THE COFFEE MIXTURE

1 tablespoon instant coffee powder or granules, dissolved in 1 tablespoon boiling water

2 tablespoons dark chocolate chips

TO FINISH

100g white chocolate, finely chopped

100ml whipping cream

cocoa powder, for dusting

1 Preheat the oven to 180°C/350°F/gas 4. Grease a 900g loaf tin (about 26 x 12.5 x 7.5cm) and line with baking paper.

2 Put the butter into a large mixing bowl. Beat using a wooden spoon or an electric mixer until very creamy. Gradually beat in the sugar, then the vanilla and keep beating for 4–5 minutes until the mixture is light and fluffy.

3 Add the eggs, a tablespoon at a time, beating well after each addition. Add 1 tablespoon of the flour with each of the last 2 portions of egg, to prevent the mixture from curdling.

4 Sift the remaining flour and the salt into the bowl and gently fold in using a large metal spoon until you can no longer see any streaks or specks of flour.

5 Transfer half the mixture to a second mixing bowl. Sift the cocoa powder onto one portion of the mixture, add the milk and fold in until completely mixed, with no streaks of cocoa. Add the cooled coffee liquid to the other portion of the mixture and stir until thoroughly combined.

6 Spoon both mixtures into the prepared tin, adding a spoonful of each alternately and scattering the chocolate chips over the mixtures between each layer. Gently bang the tin on the worktop to knock out any pockets of air, and gently smooth the surface. Marble the 2 mixtures by swirling a chopstick or round-bladed knife through.

7 Bake for 1–1¼ hours until the cake is well risen and a cocktail stick inserted into the centre comes out clean. Remove the tin from the oven and set on a wire rack and cool for 20 minutes, then carefully turn out the cake and leave to cool completely.

8 To make the ganache, put the white chocolate into a heatproof bowl. Heat the cream until hot but not boiling, then pour it slowly over the chocolate. Leave to stand for a couple of minutes, then stir gently until melted, smooth and glossy. Leave to cool and thicken before smoothing over the top of the cake. Dust with a little cocoa powder to finish.

Love Heart Biscuits

Crisp butter-rich almond biscuits are sandwiched with a fresh fruit filling – an extra-special version of jammy dodgers. The biscuit dough is easily made in a food-processor. Make romantic hearts or cut out flowers or other pretty shapes.

Makes 12

FOR THE BISCUIT DOUGH

100g unblanched almonds

200g plain flour

good pinch of salt

80g icing sugar

125g unsalted butter, chilled and diced

3 large egg yolks

FOR THE FILLING

200g raspberries

2 level teaspoons cornflour

3 level tablespoons caster sugar

icing sugar, for dusting

1 Line two baking trays with baking paper. Put the almonds, flour and salt into the bowl of a food-processor and process until the almonds are finely ground. Add the icing sugar and 'pulse' the machine a few times until combined. Add the pieces of butter and process until the mixture looks like coarse sand. Add the egg yolks and process until the mixture comes together in a ball of firm dough. Slightly flatten the ball, then wrap in clingfilm and chill for 15 minutes.

2 Roll out the dough on a lightly floured worktop to the thickness of a pound coin. Cut out shapes using a floured 8cm heart cutter (or other shapes), then use a floured smaller cutter to stamp out the middle from half of the shapes. Gather up the trimmings, re-roll and cut more hearts. Arrange them well apart on the lined baking sheets and chill for about 15 minutes.

3 Meanwhile, preheat the oven to 180°C/350°F/gas 4. Bake the biscuits for about 12 minutes until lightly coloured. If necessary, rotate the sheets halfway through baking so the biscuits cook evenly. Leave the biscuits to cool and firm up on the sheets for about 10 minutes, then transfer to a wire rack to cool completely.

4 To make the filling, put the raspberries, cornflour and caster sugar into a medium-sized pan. Set over a medium heat and stir gently until the juices start to run and the fruit softens. Bring to the boil and simmer for 2 minutes, stirring, until thick. Pour into a heatproof bowl and leave to cool.

5 To assemble, spread the cold raspberry filling over the uncut biscuits, then top each with a cut-out shape. Dust with icing sugar. Once filled, eat the biscuits the same day. (The unfilled biscuits can be stored in an airtight tin for up to 4 days, and the filling can be kept, covered, in the fridge for 4 days.)

Sticky Lemon Cake

This is a very simple all-in-one lemon cake soaked in a delicious lemon drizzle.

Makes 1 medium cake

200g unsalted butter, at room temperature

250g caster sugar

3 eggs, at room temperature

zest and juice of 2 unwaxed lemons

250g self-raising flour

½ level teaspoon baking powder

100ml milk, at room temperature

FOR THE TOPPING
100g caster sugar

1 Preheat the oven to 180°C/350°F/gas 4. Grease a 20 cm springclip or deep, round cake tin and line the base with baking paper.

2 Put the butter and sugar into a large mixing bowl and add the eggs and then the lemon zest. Sift the flour and baking powder into a bowl and then pour in the milk.

3 Set the mixing bowl on a damp towel, to prevent it from wobbling. Beat everything together with a wooden spoon or an electric mixer on medium speed. Scrape down the sides of the bowl from time to time. Stop beating as soon as the mixture looks completely smooth, with no streaks of flour or egg.

4 Scrape the mixture into the lined cake tin and spread it out evenly. Scrape down any blobs of mixture that have splashed onto the lining paper on the sides of the tin.

5 Place in the preheated oven and bake for 50–60 minutes until the cake is golden brown. To test if the cake is cooked, push a cocktail stick into the middle of the cake and if the stick comes out clean, the cake is cooked. If it comes out with sticky mix on it, put the cake back into the oven to bake for 5 more minutes, then test it again.

6 While the cake is baking, put the caster sugar for the topping into a small bowl. Add the lemon juice and stir well for a minute so the sugar just starts to dissolve to make a thick syrupy mixture.

7 Remove the tin from the oven and while the cake is still warm, use a clean cocktail stick to prick the surface all over. Quickly pour all the sugary lemon syrup over the cake. The warm cake will absorb the syrup as it cools.

8 Carefully remove the cake from the tin and peel off the lining paper. Set the cake on a serving platter or store in an airtight container at room temperature and eat within 4 days.

Aztec Cookies

These irresistible cookies, made with good dark chocolate, flavoured with real espresso coffee and full of white chocolate chunks, are a very adult treat. They taste even better the next day, if you can wait.

Makes 18

140g espresso-flavoured dark chocolate (70% cocoa solids), broken into pieces

65g unsalted butter, chilled and diced

2 large eggs, at room temperature

½ teaspoon vanilla extract

good pinch of salt

130g caster sugar

185g plain flour

1 level teaspoon baking powder

100g white chocolate

edible gold dust or glitter, to finish (optional)

1 Line two baking trays with baking paper. Melt the dark chocolate with the butter in a bowl over a pan of hot water. Remove the bowl from the pan and leave the chocolate mixture to cool for about 5 minutes until barely warm.

2 Meanwhile, put the eggs, vanilla, salt and sugar into a large mixing bowl. Using a wire whisk or hand-held electric mixer, beat for a couple of minutes until thoroughly combined. Stir in the cooled chocolate mixture.

3 Sift the flour and baking powder into the bowl and stir in using a wooden spoon. Roughly chop or break up the white chocolate into small chunks and mix in. Leave the mixture to stand for 15 minutes to firm up a bit. Meanwhile, preheat the oven to 160°C/325°F/gas 3.

4 Drop a heaped tablespoonful of mixture for each cookie onto the lined baking sheets, spacing the spoonfuls well apart to allow for spreading. Don't flatten the mixture. Bake for about 15 minutes until just set – the cookies will continue cooking for a few minutes after they come out of the oven.

5 Leave on the sheets for about 5 minutes, then transfer to a wire rack and leave to cool completely. Store in an airtight tin and eat within a week. Before serving, dust lightly with edible gold dust or edible gold glitter, if you want extra sparkle.

Simple Scones

Scones may be as old as the hills but they are still a treat eaten warm with good jam and thick cream. Any leftover scones are good split in half and toasted.

Makes 8 scones

250g self-raising flour

50g caster sugar

50g unsalted butter, cold from the fridge

3 tablespoons natural yoghurt

milk

1 egg, at room temperature, lightly beaten

1 Preheat the oven to 220°C/425°F/gas 7 and lightly grease a baking sheet. Tip the flour and sugar into a large mixing bowl. Cut the butter into small cubes about the size of your thumbnail and add to the bowl. Use the knife to toss the pieces of butter in the flour so all are coated.

2 Rub the flour and butter together using your fingertips until the mixture looks like small pieces of rubble.

3 Spoon the yoghurt into a measuring jug and pour in enough milk to measure 100ml. Add the beaten egg and mix together with a fork. Pour the egg mixture into the mixing bowl. Mix into the crumbs, first using a round-bladed knife and then, as soon as the mixture starts to stick together, using your hands.

4 Gather the dough to make a slightly soft ball. Sprinkle a little flour over the worktop, then turn out the ball of dough onto it. Gently press and squeeze the dough together for a couple of seconds just to bring it together neatly.

5 Sprinkle your hands with a little flour, then pat out the dough about 3cm thick. Dip a 6cm round cutter in flour and cut out rounds of dough. Set them, about 2cm apart, on the greased baking sheet. Press the dough scraps together and pat out again, then cut more rounds to make 8 in total.

6 Place in the preheated oven and bake for 12–15 minutes until golden brown. Remove the sheet from the oven and set on a heatproof surface. Transfer the scones to a wire rack and leave to cool slightly before serving warm. These are best eaten the same day.

Giant Cookies

These are the perfect cookies – crisp around the edges and slightly chewy in the centre, and really big!

Makes 6

125g unsalted butter, at room temperature

75g light brown muscovado sugar

75g caster sugar

½ teaspoon vanilla extract

1 egg, at room temperature, lightly beaten

150g plain flour

½ level teaspoon baking powder

PLUS 150g of your choice of extras: chocolate chips OR chopped nuts OR dried fruit OR mini sweeties

1 Preheat the oven to 180°C/350°F/gas 4 and line two baking sheets with baking paper.

2 Put the butter, both sugars and the vanilla into a large mixing bowl and beat with a wooden spoon or an electric mixer for about 2 minutes until the mixture is creamy, smooth and fluffy. Scrape down the sides of the bowl from time to time.

3 Add the egg to the butter mixture and beat well for 2 minutes, scraping down the sides of the bowl as before. Sift the flour and baking powder into the bowl and mix in with a wooden spoon until everything is completely blended.

4 Tip all of your chosen extras into the bowl and mix thoroughly into the cookie dough until they are evenly distributed – use your hands for this.

5 Divide the mixture into 6 equal portions. Using your hands, shape each into a large, rough, sticky ball (almost the size of a tennis ball) and drop onto the lined baking sheets. During baking, the mixture will spread to make cookies about 13cm across, make sure you space them well apart.

6 Place in the preheated oven and bake for 15–20 minutes until golden brown and slightly darker around the edges. Remove the baking sheets from the oven and set them on a wire rack. Leave the cookies to cool completely. Store in an airtight container and eat within 4 days.

Honeycomb Crunchies

Honeycomb is the most amazing stuff – add the bicarbonate of soda to the sugar and watch as it explodes in the pan and grows before your eyes. The honeycomb is then mixed with melted chocolate, syrup and biscuits to make a sticky, crunchy square.

Makes 16 squares

FOR THE HONEYCOMB

1 level teaspoon bicarbonate of soda

75g caster sugar

2 level tablespoons golden syrup

TO ASSEMBLE

250g dark or milk chocolate, or a mixture

100g unsalted butter, chilled and cut into 1cm cubes

2 tablespoons golden syrup

150g digestive biscuits

1 Make the honeycomb first. Have the bicarbonate of soda measured and ready for when you need it, plus a wire whisk and an oiled baking tray. Put the sugar and golden syrup into a saucepan and set it over very low heat. Warm gently for 10 minutes until all the sugar has melted, stirring occasionally with a wooden spoon.

2 When the sugar is completely melted, turn up the heat to medium. Once the mixture has started to boil, leave to bubble without stirring until it turns golden brown.

3 Turn off the heat under the pan. Cover one of your hands with an oven glove for protection, then take hold of the pan handle. Add the bicarbonate of soda and quickly whisk it in for a couple of seconds only. The mixture will froth up massively and you need to take great care as it's extremely hot.

4 Quickly pour it into the middle of the oiled baking tray. Don't spread it out or touch it or the tray. Leave it to cool and harden, which will take about 30 minutes. Line a square 20cm tin with baking paper.

5 Use a rolling pin to break up the chocolate into small pieces. Put them into a heatproof bowl and add the butter and golden syrup. Set the bowl over a pan of hot water and melt gently, giving it a stir now and then. When the chocolate mixture is smooth, carefully lift the bowl off the pan and set it on a heatproof surface.

6 Put the biscuits into a plastic bag, tie loosely, and use the rolling pin to break them up into chunks the size of your thumbnail. Bash the set honeycomb into chunks roughly the same size. Add the biscuits and honeycomb to the melted chocolate and mix well until all the chunks are coated.

7 Scoop the whole lot into the lined tin and spread it evenly, right into the corners. Cover with clingfilm, then chill in the fridge for about 2 hours until firm and set. Cut into 16 squares using a sharp knife. Store, tightly covered, in the fridge and eat within 2 days.

THANK YOU

A big thank you to the brilliant people who helped
put this little book together:

Maja Smend, Chris Terry, Dan Jones and Cristian Barnett,
Bobby Birchall, Stephanie Evans, Helen Everson, Muna Reyal,
Laura Higginson, Kevin Cahill, Anne-Cecile Berthier,
Lou Wickstead, Tom Hemsley, Lucille Flood, Trevor Leighton,
Rick Scott, Letty Kavanagh and Amanda Westwood.

Published in 2013 by BBC Books, an imprint of Ebury
Publishing. A Random House Group company.

Recipes by Linda Collister © Love Productions
Photography by Cristian Barnett and Dan Jones © Woodlands
Books Ltd and © Maja Smend and Chris Terry.
Photography on pages 1, 3, 4 and 5 © Comic Relief 2012.
Design by Bobby Birchall. © Woodlands Books Ltd

All the recipes in this book were taken from *The Great British
Bake Off: How to Bake; How to Turn Everyday Bakes into
Showstoppers;* and *Learn to Bake*, first published in August
2011, August 2012 and October 2012.

Printed by Marstan Press

Comic Relief, registered charity 326568 (England/Wales);
SCO39730 (Scotland)